For

BIRDS
— OF A —
FEATHER

Compiled by
Jennifer Bryant

PETER PAUPER PRESS, INC.

WHITE PLAINS, NEW YORK

For Anna
Copyright © 1993
Peter Pauper Press, Inc.
202 Mamaroneck Avenue
White Plains, NY 10601
All rights reserved
ISBN 0-88088-761-3
Printed in Singapore
7   6   5   4   3   2   1

CONTENTS

INTRODUCTION

Though we seldom take the time to appreciate them, birds play an undeniable role in the symbolism of our daily lives. Many of our most significant beginnings and endings are punctuated by the appearance of our feathered friends: the rooster's insistent crow at dawn, the first robin of spring, the last flock of winter geese, the life-bringing stork and the ominous circling vultures of death.

Birds' capacity for flight gives them a transcendent quality which we earth-bound humans often envy. He "flew the coop," she "took off," we say when people successfully shed their everyday obligations.

But perhaps birds' most important contribution is themselves. Bird-watching, if only for a moment, can be an effective antidote to the stresses and strains of modern living. When we listen to the soothing refrain of the mourning dove or the playful chirping of the chickadees, or watch brightly-colored cardinals gather at the backyard feeder, we leave technology behind and participate once again in the beauty and simplicity of nature.

J. B.

QUOTATIONS

If you want to see birds, you must have birds in your heart.

John Burroughs

Among the artistic hierarchy, birds are probably the greatest musicians to inhabit our planet.

Olivier Messiaen

A bird came down the walk:
He did not know I saw;
He bit an angle-worm
* in halves*
And ate the fellow, raw.
                    Emily Dickinson

You must hear the bird's song without attempting to render it into nouns and verbs.

Ralph Waldo Emerson

Man feels himself an infinity above those creatures who stand, zoologically, only one step below him, but every human being looks up to the birds.

Donald Culross Peattie

So many people feel a sense of affinity and recognition with birds. Our admiration for their bright colors, sweet songs, and graceful flight suggests that some very large part of our brains is still up in the canopy with them . . .

David Rains Wallace

Once a Zen master stood up before his students and was about to deliver a sermon. And just as he was about to open his mouth, a bird sang. And he said, "The sermon has been delivered."

Joseph Campbell

Birds are Nature's most vital and potent expressions.
Frank M. Chapman

I know why the caged bird sings.
Paul Laurence Dunbar

*Describe underwater swim-
ming and you will have
described the flight of birds.*
  Leonardo da Vinci

*Birds of a feather flock
together.*

  Aristotle

*Getting up too early is a
vice habitual in horned
owls, stars, geese and freight
trains.*

Aldo Leopold

A jay is a bird of the crow family, which can be found in fields and meadows. A jaywalker, on the other hand, is a bird of the Schmoe family who can be found in traffic jams and morgues.

Phyllis Battelle

Protect the birds. The dove brings peace and the stork brings tax exemptions.

Birmingham News

When I was a kid, singing groups were named after such things as birds: we had the Ravens, the Robins, and the Orioles. But only the Vultures or the Pigeon Droppings could be singing groups today.

Bill Cosby

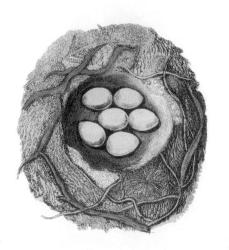

It is better to be a young June-bug than an old bird of paradise.

Mark Twain

If we have as much sense as geese, we will stay in formation with those who are ahead of where we want to go and be willing to accept their help as well as give ours to others.

Angeles Arrien,
Quoted by Darrell Sifford

The structure of a play is always the story of how the birds came home to roost.
Arthur Miller

It is not only fine feathers that make fine birds.
Aesop

I am the kind of man who would never notice an oriole building a nest unless it came and built it in my hat in the hat room of the club.
Stephen Leacock

I was walking my dog in Prospect Park in Brooklyn one recent morning when I heard a wolf whistle from above. I looked up and saw a starling that had interrupted its apartment house construction to (I presumed) admire my style.

Jane E. Brody

If you cannot catch a bird of paradise, better take a wet hen.

Nikita Khrushchev

*There are three classes
which need sanctuary more
than others—birds, wild
flowers, and Prime Ministers.*
Stanley Baldwin

The eagle has ceased to scream, but the parrots will now begin to chatter.
Winston Churchill,
on V-E Day, May 7, 1945

Over increasingly large areas of the United States, spring now comes unheralded by the return of the birds, and the early mornings are strangely silent where once they were filled with the beauty of bird song.

Rachel Carson,
Silent Spring

*Birds . . . are sensitive
indicators of the environment,
a sort of "ecological litmus
paper" . . . The observation
of birds leads inevitably to
environmental awareness.*
Roger Tory Peterson

Seeing this gradation and diversity of structure in one small, intimately related group of birds, one might really fancy that from an original paucity of birds in this archipelago, one species had been taken and modified for different ends.

Charles Darwin,
on evolution

Birds, even the prettiest of them, are little savages. . . . I cannot help noticing how ungenerously they behave toward one another . . .
                    John Burroughs

The struggle for life among the birds . . . is so severe that the feeble and malformed, or the handicapped in any way, quickly drop out. . . . They are always in the enemy's country; they are always on the firing-line; eternal vigilance and ceaseless activity are the price of life with them.

John Burroughs

*One touch of nature makes
the whole world kin; and it
is truly wonderful how love-
telling the small voices of
these birds are, and how far
they reach through the
woods into one another's
hearts and into ours.*

John Muir

Your first observations of birds and their behavior can be done by simply learning to drift gently through a wood: a naturalist in a hurry never learns anything of value.

Gerald Durrell

Birding . . . is not just a hobby to fill in the empty hours. It is a way of life, in tune with the total natural scene. Call it an addiction if you like; but it is a benign addiction from which great blessings flow.

Lola Oberman

Birds are thoughts and flights of the mind.

Carl Jung

I'm no Roger Tory Peterson, but I do enjoy watching birds.

Senator Lloyd Bentsen

A bird can fly where it wants to when it wants to. I am sure that is what appealed to me when I was in school. Regimentation and restriction rubbed me the wrong way . . . There were times when I wished that I could fly as they did and leave everything.

Roger Tory Peterson

I find it hard to see anything about a bird that it does not want seen. It demands my full attention.

Annie Dillard

*It seemed to me, separated
from my own species, that I
was nearer to others: the
shy willet, nesting in the
ragged tide-wash behind me;
the sand piper, running in
little unfrightened steps
down the shining beach rim
ahead of me . . . I felt a kind
of impersonal kinship with
them and a joy in that
kinship.*

Anne Morrow Lindbergh
Gift From The Sea

Red headed Linnet Nest & Eggs.

Red Headed Linnet.

*Birds migrate every year to
the four corners of the globe
just like their dinosaur
forefathers used to roam the
entire world millions of
years ago.*

narrated by
Walter Cronkite

I fairly ache to stroke the silky feathers on throat and brow, to feel the beat of wild hearts lose their fear-driven throb under my friendly touch. . . . These things fascinate me, just as the touch of a human hand seems to fascinate some of the bird folk.

Ada Clapham Govan

*For life is more than
food . . . Consider the ravens;
they neither sow nor reap,
and they have neither
storehouse nor barn, and yet
God feeds them. Of how
much more value are you
than the birds!*

Luke 12:23-24

*[There] came a Dove flying
to the shippe, being Good
Friday at Sunsett; and sat
him on the Shippe-top;
whereat they were all
comforted, and tooke it for a
miracle and good token . . .
and all gave heartie thanks
to God, directing our course
the way the Dove flew.*

Hernando Cortez,
*record of his first
voyage to America*

*The Humbird is one of the
wonders of the country,
being no bigger than a
hornet, yet hath all the
dimensions of a bird, a bill
and wings, with quills,
spider-like legs, small claws;
for colors, she is glorious as
the rainbow . . .*

William Wood

Take a close look at Crow. The first thing you will note about him is his color—coal black from bill to tail-tip. It's as if he decided a long time ago that suiting up in colorful or cryptic garb was a waste of time better spent snooping about for a free feed.

Charles Fergus

They that hurt robins
or wrens
Will never prosper, boys
or men.

Cornwall Proverb

I value my garden more for being full of blackbirds than of cherries, and very frankly give them fruit for their songs.

Joseph Addison,
The Spectator

*True hope is swift, and flies
with swallow's wings;
Kings it makes gods and
meaner creatures kings.*

Shakespeare,
King Richard III

Swans sing before they die;
*   'twere no bad thing*
Should certain persons die
*   before they sing.*
        Samuel Taylor Coleridge

Green Wren Nest & Eggs.

Green Wren.

The proud sun-loving
peacock with his feathers,
   Walks all alone, thinking
   himself a king.
And with his voice
prognosticates all weathers,
   Although God knows
   how badly doth he sing . . .
                    Author Unknown

I heard a bird sing
    In the dark of December
A magical thing
    And sweet to remember.
"We are nearer to Spring
    Than we were in
    September,"
I heard a bird sing
    In the dark of December.

Oliver Herford

He clasps the crag with
  crooked hands;
Close to the sun in lonely
  lands,
Ring'd with the azure world,
  he stands.

The wrinkled sea beneath
  him crawls;
He watches from his
  mountain walls,
And like a thunderbolt
  he falls.

Alfred, Lord Tennyson,
The Eagle

*A bird in the hand is worth
two in the bush.*
Miguel de Cervantes

*The bird of paradise alights
only upon the hand that
does not grasp.*
John Berry

Then the little Hiawatha
Learned of every bird its
  language,
Learned their names and all
  their secrets,
How they built their nests
  in Summer;
Where they hid themselves
  in Winter,
Talked with them whene'er
  he met them. . . .

Henry Wadsworth
Longfellow,
The Song of Hiawatha

BIRD FACTS

A hummingbird, because
of its extraordinarily high
metabolism, must eat
almost constantly or risk
death from starvation in
just a few hours.

Birds and humans are
the only creatures on
earth who regularly walk
in the upright position.

The largest living bird is the ostrich of North Africa; it can grow to a height of 9 feet and a weight of nearly 350 pounds. It takes roughly 40 minutes to boil an ostrich egg, and although the shell is just 6/100 of an inch thick, it can support the weight of a 280-pound man.

The smallest living bird is
the bee hummingbird,
which measures only
2.24 inches in length and
weighs 6/10 of an ounce.

Chickens are by far the most abundant domesticated birds. It has been estimated that there are 1.6 chickens for every person living today.

Wheat Ear Nest & Eggs.

Wheat Ear.

The last known example
of the rare dusky sea
sparrow died at Disney
World in Orlando, Florida,
in May, 1987. A sample
of its tissue was frozen,
however, so that future
technology might permit
it to be genetically cloned.

Cliff-dwelling peregrine falcons are world-renowned for their incredible diving speed. They have been clocked regularly at speeds of 150 miles or more with the record standing at 217 mph.

Primitive man often used
bird feathers as insulation
against the cold.

Some of the smaller
migrating bird species
nearly double their
weight in preparation for
their grueling journey.
Some scientists think that
this weight increase
actually signals the
migration to begin.

Most birds sleep by
tucking their beak under
a wing and pulling one
foot up underneath their
body. This is done to
minimize heat loss from
those areas not insulated
by feathers.

The great artist Leonardo da Vinci studied bird anatomy and movement in great detail. In his notes, he recorded the mechanics of flight: "Air that is struck with greatest velocity of motion condenses the most . . . it then becomes dense as a cloud."

The first feathered bird
was Archeopteryx (mean-
ing "ancient wing")
which appeared on earth
150 million years ago. Its
skeleton was found in
Bavaria, southern
Germany, in 1861.

The now-famous dodo bird was discovered by the Dutch on the island of Mauritius in 1598. Before man, it had no natural predators and the female laid only one egg each year. By 1700, however, the dodo was extinct due to human capture and consumption.

Ninety per cent of all of
the animal extinctions on
earth have been birds.